Waking in the Light

Waking in the Light
A Lenten Journey

Devotional Poems

Ariana D. Den Bleyker

RESOURCE *Publications* • Eugene, Oregon

WAKING IN THE LIGHT
A Lenten Journey

Resource Publications
An Imprint of Wipf and Stock Publishers
199 W. 8th Ave., Suite 3
Eugene, OR 97401

www.wipfandstock.com

PAPERBACK ISBN: 979-8-3852-2519-4
HARDCOVER ISBN: 979-8-3852-2520-0
EBOOK ISBN: 979-8-3852-2521-7

VERSION NUMBER 07/02/24

For Jim & Phyllis O'Connell

Contents

Acknowledgments

First and foremost, I would like to praise and thank God the Almighty who has granted the countless blessings, knowledge, and opportunity that enabled me to share these words.

Many thanks to the following pastors whose sermons during The Reformed Churches of the Wallkill Valley 2024 Lenten Worship Series (Sabbath as Resistance) provided great inspiration for many of the poems in this collection: James O'Connell of The First Reformed Church of Walden, NY; Irving Rivera of Meadow Hill Reformed Church; Stan Seagren of The Wallkill Reformed Church; Gary Sissel of The Gardiner Reformed Church; and, Howie Dalton, Pastor Emeritus, The Wallkill Reformed Church.

Much gratitude and love to James O'Connell whose daily devotions throughout Lent inspired many of these poems and whose love and guidance have spiritually nourished me for twenty years.

To Phyllis O'Connell whose friendship has blessed me with kindness, support, love, and guidance, and taught me what it means to be a true child of Christ for so, so many years.

Finally, to my church family, for making every day feel like Sunday in my heart.

Ash Wednesday

That ashes come from fire—soft black thick-smoke soot of earth—powder once firm green frond, bright & vibrant before dry & brittle, stiff & fibrous before flame transforms it into dust. That every living thing submits to change, our breathing a journey from death into life—second by second, prayer by prayer. Do not fear it—that change. That from seed to plant, palm to ash, this earth imposed on our foreheads by the hands of God as we walk into fire, as we become ash to ash & dust to dust, covers us with cloak, brings us low to the earth, the power of forgiveness deep in our bones; covers us with darkness, leaves us praying & weeping, groaning in our singing, longing to be heard into being, stretching beyond breathing; and, covers us with His mercy, the bones He has crushed rejoicing. Cover us with ash—bring us to our knees, so that in our weakness, we see Your strength, the reflection of Your eyes inside our brokenness, the fullness of Your love inside our hearts. Cover us. Change us.

Our Yoke to Bear

Matthew 11:25-30

& in the garden on the Seventh day, we rested in peace with God until our restlessness stole our rest within Him; but, tonight, we turn our faces toward Him to see upon Christ's shoulders a yoke that is not a yoke, a yoke lined with love—we walk in unison, young & unlearned, loosening burden from our shoulders, shedding trouble & worry, our heavy load, our hearts tick-tocking between two poles & with each step two great pails brimming with honey & milk—cows' mother-soul, the foam of chewed grass gushing in soft streams down our bodies. I am the servant girl of the farm ploughing; I stride in length of my pain with each firm step. His pail is full of blood, & I drink my fill of that life & take of God's salvation, for the fields are full to harvest & the fruit of it still calls—for His yoke is easy & His burden light. Let us rest without resistance. Let us rest in His arms tonight.

Blessings on the Mountaintop

Matthew 5:1-12

I want to climb Your mountain, soft & gray, slowly, sleep on the bare rock You sit upon, look back at everything—peaceful—You no longer belonging to the past but living in the present, the everlasting today of God, perhaps in the exaggerated grace of Your weight settling, wings raised, whose feathers come away in my hands—oh, but don't pull apart. Even before You were with me, even before You were in me, song was all we had—here I am as I've been, here before, & before You began to speak without sound. Perfect stillness. I thank You when I have finally found Your face because now I can see the blessings & all I will ever need.

Waking in the Light

John 1:5

I shiver beneath shuddering clouds shaking loose the long, cold stare of February darkness. I smell the coming snow, the break in the clouds, the slivered moon. In this darkness, I am trembling; in this crack of moon, I am reborn. There in no heartbeat in seed, yet life awaits surely as in the stilled breathing & slowed beating hearts of bears in winter caves—waiting, waiting—just as we wait in lengthened nights & chilled soil for warmer, lighter, moister days, pulsing in the depths, hearing, *Be still, I'm coming—I did. I am. I will.* If I say please, will You hold my hand? God, take my hand. You are here now to toss soil, to remind me of what you've allowed me to become when all I could do was cry, assured that as I hold, I will be held.

Do Not Worry

Matthew 6:25-34

The sun throws beams against the cliffs, through narrow cliffs, & widening caves, & the manna falls, pouring down its balm to put worry to rest inside His rest, a space of quiet for simple being & letting be, for learning how to live again. That we are made from earth & it from our bodies. The birds of the air fly in us; we see the arc of their flight & we fly & we are fed. I have heard in that rare silence the low, soft voice of God reach out His hand to cup my heart.

A Firm Foundation

Matthew 7:24-25

The small space I was born into has not stayed the same. Home changes, but You took my flesh from the clay that came from everywhere & formed me into the weathered stone hidden in the waters. Your Word is fastened to the sky, a great nail bolstering this house into white stars through the midnight blue. There are stars in my bones & oceans in my blood. I press my palm into my chest in the blustering salt wind & say a prayer for the steel spikes of Your love driving me into You.

Remember to Give Thanks

Psalm 22:27

Though the night is still for sleep & dreaming, I hear Him calling. So I listen. I wait. I rise. Hear the whistle blowing, the metal speeding through the dense, dark night. It speaks of the Spirit spreading inside me, curls a last bend, settles soft within—my spirit its worn tracks; my heart its worn rumble. The minutes pass by. The minutes never pass by. Inch by inch, mile by mile, all narrow tracks lead to His arrival, & in the end I stand upon that platform & give thanks for the valleys lifted despite everything.

Crocus in Late Winter

1 Corinthians 3:7

I bloom, push forth my blades, each new leaf, miracle of thaw, a seed broken by sun & water, a sweep of the tree swaying above me, the deep rustling of evergreen a message of presence, of being—hidden strength. This canopy of branches, His bark folding itself into gnarled whorls speaks of aging rings & steadfast love. We are rooted together—still—making channels through this earth, & I am struck by my true place of be-longing, the ever-patient peace of the seed of God inside me.

Take This Seed

Matthew 17:20

I stretch my hands from fists & spread them palm up to the skies,
& in my left palm a tiny mustard seed. You say this seed moves
mountains. Move this mountain for me. I'm hungry, & I hold this
tiny seed. Take my seed & fill me. Heal my unbelief until the earth
quakes & I feel the sharpest edges wash away.

The Bread Is Hungry Here

Matthew 4:1-11

Let me inhale the heaviness of Your silence, the light clean on the shape of Your neck. Forty days in the wilderness of deep sun & deep sky—dust & swirling wind where temptation lives, wild & yearning, You walk with bleeding feet, burning throat, ache & spit, cracked lips & trembling limbs, belly pregnant with emptiness; I fast with You in my thirst for Your salvation—reach for Your warm hand resting on my shoulder & know that I am known inside the deep sound of Your love.

A New Commandment

John 13:34-35

& in the perfect garden we excluded ourselves from God, & he lifted His head, stilled us, sent us Noah to wash away the sin, Moses to lead, John to remind, Jesus to forgive. Love & peace are holy. God, the creator, the life table. God, the ocean with all its creations; peace the falcon flying over Him, catching the fish swimming in Him; God, the order of being, the tree on the embankment, the reef, the screaming wind creating clouds, the hurricane coming to shore, the rest on the Seventh day. I catch water in my hands—running water, raining water, soapy water, staining water—pooling into my hands. You can hear God in water. He calls & I come, opening a space within myself formed of peace, laid bare in sunlight, compelled to look inward to ask do I love my home, these things, this family, others, myself? When our stiff necks have softened, when we love one another, there falls a stillness upon us, & a great voice says find rest in my heart & a song of praise on your lips—*Shalom. Shalom Alchechem.*

Taking Up the Cross

Mark 8:34

Take up your cross, deny yourself & follow, let its weight carry you. I will pray into the marrow of my bones, into the crevices of the lifelines of my hands. I will lift the timber, & when I see the beam upended, the rugged post pointing to the sky, the crossbar running from side to side, I'll remember arms opened wide. & as the soil freshens, my dragging cross furrowing the earth, & in its harrow hope growing as though its phantom roots burrow, I'll look back with firm eyes saying this is where I want to go. I want to melt into that fierce heart of the dying, falling toward the center of my longing. I have heard in that fiery embrace God can change you. & I will open my arms to the dying, to the fragile beauty of God so that as I step toward Him, I know deep in the heart of the cross nothing is lost.

Be the Light

Matthew 5:14

The city on the hill has walls that are not walls, its tree-bowered streets peace in the love that is the city singing while it sleeps, a city set against a sky so saturated with twilight hanging in air, blessed— watch the wind press down the trees & the trees rise against the wind & the moon. & yet beyond this quiet scene the morning hangs in the air, hovering slowly, turning, settling down like flakes sifting onto the city, & a faithful sun's dawning light rises ageless across the night, a light divided from darkness familiar as prayer. But it has not risen because we've seen it, but because by it, we see all things illuminated with brightness & beauty. That we find Him standing upright in the light living inside the light we share with others in the deepest dark. Make a place where the day speaks to the night; gather the light in imperfect hands & throw it into the wind.

God Is Like the Sun

Psalm 19

Throughout our years, the sidelong hip of the Milky Way—the sun, the moon, the stars—God's silent poetry, timeless Word, beauty eternal, His wonders unfurled from His hands, shows itself to us. We see backward across years along the light of His work. The sky & the screaming birds & all their fullness sing: *Holy, holy, holy.* We hear the Word in the wind, face the stars & wait. The sun bursts with joy & strength; it springs from the mouth of the sky & lights the whole of the heavens. Nothing is hidden from its heat. My chest, my ribs fill with the breath that made them. Let me join the angels in this ancient sky—let the music of my heart draw me back & bring Him delight.

Turn to God

Psalm 25

Sometimes the deepest, most tender love feels fragile, & you need it to last because it's vulnerable & wouldn't be love otherwise. & sometimes, the deepest, most tender love frightens. Through hills & valleys, & fields that burn, we follow You faithfully. Teach us. Take us, Lord. Take all of us, take what You have given us. I'm not holding anything back & I seek You. I lift my eyes to You. With You, I'm laid bare, an open book written in a language only You can translate & it scares me. I'm soft & vulnerable, but my trust outweighs my fears. You peel rough layers from me with a warmth & patience so nurturing it tames me. You are a fire igniting a lost soul in the darkest of places; You give me hidden treasures & forgiveness, treasures only found in the illumination of trust & comfort. I turn to You, permanently unpeeled & open & sing; let this be my prayer to you.

He Knows What's In You

John 2:13-22

Hope is perched on my lips, slippery on my tongue, lodged beneath my heart, gnawing at my gut—it's everywhere behind the turbulence of this moment, absorbed in the dark, the light. If I could hold my breath in water, smell the burning fire, hear the crackling beneath Your voice—even as the stars disappear in the presence of the sun, You fade into me & I am full. I think of which angers have been Your anger, of Your joy, mine, all along knowing I've been burying my feet in the dirt, staring at olive trees, waiting for bushes to burn. That it's safe in this moment with You to weigh my thoughts, knowing some tables need turning, & pour my words just as they are, certain Your faithful hand will take & sift them, keep what's worth keeping, & blow the rest away.

When Roots Run Deep

Colossians 2:6-7

My roots anchor deep into the ground, packed firm & damp with living water & soil, the strength of the tree above me growing in a green meadow, a willow or birch, oak or pine bowing often, light flowing from its branches—soft & wet & hushed—where chickadees are building nests, weaving & hollowing them, hanging them safe on the topmost limbs, offshoots of Heaven—creation itself, the renewing power of stillness, faith in the magic of rest, in Sabbath, hope in the roots that are long & deep, whose shoots recur fresh & green, love of the law of eternal delight, love of what is, love that is not oppressive, freedom—a guiltless moment of reflection, of fixing the broken, of grace & forgiveness & solace, of hearing the care of God, experiencing a work of grace, finding again a song of thankfulness in the night, in the stars, in the building of faith.

What Has He Done?

John 3:14

When the day breaks & the brazen sun stands as if to say the storm has passed once more, I lay in a whisper of suffering, fists clenching & unclenching, silence so deafening I ache, suffering my home, the rays hurling themselves around me & a fiery snake sunning at my feet, jaw unhinged, lapping up my sin like crimson rain, tongue a black arrow. I turn up into the orange light, to the bronze snake hovering above me in the sky, its copper belly redemption breathing life into me. I stand with the crowd being healed in the wilderness—we stand, our eyes turned up to the sun, to the broken body lifted, hanging heavy, heart a wound opened wide with welcome for all those who have their weary hands within its messy flow—holiness & grace & forgiveness colliding with fire.

Steadfast Love

Psalm 107

Thank you for the bones you've molded in me to brave every un-settling so they may hold tight & listen—that the desert always thickens, the remnants of stars paving the way for another day of stubborn sun before a wind announces a storm to the east & strange birds fall out of the sky; that we always cage ourselves awaiting thunder to splinter us, noises of pain seeping through shackles reaching our own hurt, breaking our bones to dredge sadness from our chests, the darkness welcoming us into a world unknown, its hands bound so tightly around our wrists; that we always tuck beneath white sheets as we cough, as we fall, in all sickness, every blush conjuring fever, fever so high we hear the shapeless voices of dark angels; that we always seek the albatross soaring above the green water subsuming us, bodies tossed in storm, exhausting breath into the winter surge amid the break-ers—how fearful is the tumult, the cry, the shriek, the prayer in this raging sea until the morning calm comes & blinds us with light in darkness until we are the light, & link by link, together we forge a chain, a long string of light braided into a ray that God bends in the palm of His hand into a floating sun of steadfast love we lift in our praise & song.

Alive in Christ

Ephesians 2:1-10

& when the universe was shaped by the power of His Word & breath of His Spirit, He spoke & called forth life, exhaled & the Spirit floated over the waters. & when He took the dust & formed the foundation—Creator, Word, Spirit—He bathed the universe in its tenderness, poured it over what was raw & new & soft & still. Before His breath became our breath, He took His hands & cradled our heads, our fullness of being chosen seamless. Tonight, I inhale the Word in flesh, take from an overflowing cup & drink of its salvation. I breathe deep, unravel the Word inside me, grateful & patient with even breath, understanding what I've heard my whole life about the faithful finding life in Christ.

When Life Falls Apart

Psalm 46

I will build my home in God & paint its walls yellow with peace & protection. & I will not fear catastrophe. & I will be blessed with an abundance of water, an ever-rainy spring. & I will drink from the stream, drink deep from Him, quench my thirst in the Spirit, the well within me & find joy amid turbulence. I will not be broken. I will rejoice, for the Lord is my strength. & I will be still, let go, put my hands down, & know He is with me, always.

What Is This Thing Called Love?

John 3:16-17

You gave Him to us. You left Him with us. Your Word became flesh, lifting us up & enfolding us in sun-drenched wings, pulling us up into the sky, setting us free, the wind carrying us forward, surrounding us with peace, our strength a seed of hope bathed in light. & we are carried by You, Your talons digging deep into the river, or that soft, green dark valley; we feel You breathe in the whole world, Your love woven & strong, connecting & filling the universe, lighting the stars, knowing no boundaries. & the seed perpetually seeking the light blossoms, branches thickening, strengthening dividing, reaching into the place that was once too dark, heavy, & in time, bore fruit—its beauty held it the grace of the death of Him in its arms.

Who Are We in a Hurry to Meet?

Matthew 6:24-34

We sit, snagged by the collective weight of time, its downward pull, its structure of our lives bending against the days, us floating on the surface at war with ourselves with distraction, forgetting to watch the sun set or the rain fall, the clouds drifting overhead—to be what we are doing with our whole hearts. Lift the brilliant drop of water rolling along the tongue of a green leaf & you'll find God, the very tree whose crown rises higher than we can see; but we reach high & touch the wrong sun, unable to slow down, stretching thin & stuffing full, letting the temporal capture the longing, unaware our presence is God's present. The birds take turns with their evening songs filled with no worry, fully alive, finding rest just as the Sabbath gives us rest, hope in possibility, healing & freedom. When dawn unwraps itself & we awaken & the Earth changes & home becomes different places, let us learn not to worry about dark mysteries & inexhaustible days within our twin & triple selves—let us find sacred space instead, a cathedral of sun & stillness & keep it holy & surrender the weight.

Create in Me a Clean Heart

Psalm 51:1-12

Dirt gathers slowly & blackens the window until the dark glass cracks & sun blazes through & all I see is the darkness left inside me, as if every hollow reflection holds past shame no matter where it's buried—so many things no one sees except You. Although the faults inside my eyes remain mistakes—once, twice, now, & again—over time, these shackles will wither into rust, letting their weight crumble, & I will vibrate like a fish bone caught in a throat crying out for You until all I can feel is my breathing, & I'll remember how human & animal-like I am, & know I am forgiven. & my bruised bones will dance away their reddish sadness & my hard yet changeable heart will squeeze into summer stark as daisies in the moonlight. Take me, bind me close. Break me, & I'll become nothing again, & on my lips will swell a song I'll sing & sing, my sacrifice a broken spirit only You can love.

To Live, You Must Die

John 12:24-25

Hear the wind's low murmur in the rippled wheat, the warm breath it blows, watch the slender heads droop in prayer—how their dust fills your mouth, how your sweat draws in the cracked husks. Breathe slow & long into all this ripening. Be humble before it—this tiniest stone lying in wait for rain, leaning into the sun, wild seed making roots from water, a tending of soft beginning—tenderness, grace locked in a swollen grain & with the shedding of its husk, a new birth. Feel dusk roll in, low & brown, a golden evening where all your silos are full & the wind is whispering of the bread broken for you.

Rejoice & Be Glad

Psalm 118

His kindness ripples, a language lifting the fallen & mending the broken, a testament of love held out in His hand forever. I reach across the river from the gorge of a landslide to Him standing at the crest of a typhoon & He lifts me up & sets me in an open field. I delight in the wide-open space, the way an endless carpet of pines in the distance & cloud shadows stand still. He is with me & there is no void in the openness, only hope & refuge. & even when hornets descend seeking blood, there is nothing but the fog of smoke & a cloud of wasps falling from His lips. Even though I've suffered a hundred stings, in the silence of the minute, I can inhale the sun. The air is so clean I can take in the universe with my lungs, expanding me, forcing me alive—to know that I am nothing & He is my song sharpening a gate hinge opening towards home. & I will enter & find a stone, dappled gray, edges age-worn, rough, alone, tossed out, though solid enough, becoming the one to build a house safe from the night, the cornerstone keeping me—home. This is a day the Lord has made—the asters shake from stem to flower as the monarchs arrive, every butterfly knowing the ways we are transformed. Let Him exhale a breath of crimson into the twilight, break His blessing over me. Let peace fall in a sigh from my lips, rise as praise from my throat, & sound as song for Him forever.

For in This Hope We Are Saved

Romans 8:18-25

I hold my face in my hands, hold my face to keep the pain warm—two hands protecting, nourishing, preventing my spirit from leaving me in anger. Nothing wants to suffer—not the wind scraping itself against the cliff or the cliff being eaten by the sea. But it is when I am hollowed with knives, suffering carved deep inside my belly, winnowing room for joy, I remember suffering & joy are crops prepared on a hearth & set on a table, & at this table we sing with joy, with sorrow. We pray of suffering. We wait & give thanks for we've been rewarded. We eat the sun, ensconced in its brilliance, looking down on us, so far beyond reach, drink it from that exhale of gold. I want to stir myself into the universe freshly created, still warm like blood—no outer space, just Him, the light of all the not-yet stars drifting like a bright mist, & all of us, & everything with & within Him holding me tightly to His chest so that my flesh may break & my stone crack with its heart standing in the sun. I want to feel the press of the wind in my throat, light candles & pray for buried things to rise in the raw dawn where roots delve deep & a spark ignites—light extending its wings, taking to the sky in song. Who would have guessed it possible the waiting is sustainable & hope is a place with its own harvest?

The Promise of a New Day

Jeremiah 31:31-34

The grid of ribbed light slipping under the water as the full tide slides into little stream-cut creeks is the slender forefinger of God touching the blue rib of my storm-broken body. This soft light of a new morning binds us—oh the high arching of ribs everywhere over my hot, slack belly, how they cradle my heart, its thick clutch of muscle tender & unbroken rising under the bones that shield it. I lie on sand in the washed light & feel Him with me, within me, His promise caged inside me, its plume & beating & song everything I need to remember I am forgiven at every sun rise.

Faith in a Dark World

Isaiah 50:4-11

I walk with You in the dark; it is loud & holds us tightly. Lord, meet me in the moment in the quiet of this place—help me hear Your voice alone. Awaken & open my ear & I will listen, take it in, work it out over the rolls of my tongue. Your Word will flow my lips, & from behind my eyes, You will smile upon the earth. Let me be the lion stalking its prey wanting ease & a tender animal in its mouth to take its hunger, let the ache burn until the flame rages so brightly my body becomes glass, glimpsing its own face in the light. Let me burn myself in a fire that warms everyone & engulfs me until I melt & scatter among the weary, never doubting in the dark what You have given me in the light.

When Darkness Comes

Psalm 31:9-16

You've built Your house within my bones with Your hands. A new house, standing warm with staring window & wide-open door. It settles down on its haunches, suns itself & sleeps in the stillness of night. You raise me up in Your hand, guard me with something stronger than the heart—a whirring felt deep in the body. Let me hide in the rooms of this house, in You, unashamed—wrap Your walls inside & around me & hear me, have pity for the name Your lips form for me. You know my fear because You have hung in my place, & I've cried for the hollowness inside me, unable to escape the years. Make all the things that hunt me slip soundlessly into hungry ground. I see their fear—a dread stretching behind me & they scatter & turn away. I will not dwell in a grave made for the dead by the living. All these worries run inside the circle of Your hand. Bathe me in light. Warm me. Save me because You love me.

Emptying

Philippians 2:5-11

I want to open these knots, shed them, give them back to the air, intricate & breakable, exist between earth & sky, raw & unfiltered beyond & within, so full I must brim, reach, spill, carry in capillaries in endless emptying & resurrection. Make me empty, until, for rejoicing, a space large enough to echo Your name appears inside my bones & I rise. Here, this ache becomes the way the hollow obtains hallowing—that Your death offers comfort & consolation, a deep tremor, the trembling of a fullness drawing near. That I will cling to rocks, soak in sunlight, absorb water, float in a pool of being—feeling emptying & follow You until the sun fades into a fishbowl of stars, swimming in black velvet night.

Scar on the Cheek

Mark 14:10-11

I've sold You for thirty pieces & kissed You with a mouth to breathe in every shade of yellow, its swift plant burning long & thin, dripping red on black dirt, the red blooming anew, transforming into wild, vibrant roses. & You did not push me away, breathe too heavily, embrace less sincerely; my betrayal utters itself against Your body—I've swallowed the silver, the flesh & blood. I've counted every piece of silver over & over again until my mouth ached when I coughed those coins into the night. There is hurt surprise when morning's ruddy promise dies, when the yellowing bruise begins fading, when I find the grace formed on your lips asking me again if I love You & You show me Your scar.

Peace Be With You

John 14:27

I stumble upon the stillness of the forest after rain, upon that vast gentle conversation, Heaven to earth, & hold the curve of my own face with the same reverence I hold for You, close my eyes & feel at the center of my core the peace You left me. Peace inside me. Peace around me: the river & its long white stroke of roiling & continuous surge, the grass, gone to seed, wavering in the wind, then stilling, wavering, then stilling, my own body unmoving in the breeze. It feels good in this moment to be more tree than cloud, more silence than song. That this peace cannot be known except in the words of its making, its presence a pulse, a vibration of Your gentle light.

Triumph & Tears

Luke 19:28-40

& they shout in that sweet, fierce hour, laying cloaks & palms at Your feet—the fronds rising & curling in the open air, bathing in the blueness of sky. & I join with them in song, sending my voice in search of clouds deep enough to hold my *hosannas* as Your colt ploughs cracked earth with its dusty hooves under the gold cape of sun splayed across this space full of howling people whose eyes brim with thirst & fever. & I, trembling woman kneeling before You, fold & bend my fronds, look to You & weep, watch Your lips with expectation as You pass me—drop my branches as You enter into this broken city, everyone waiting for You to save them, expecting Jerusalem to be Your kingdom & nothing more, & yet still You move forward riding tenderly, one dirty hoof after another, brave.

His Tears Are For You

Luke 19:41-44

That You regard us with tears, wells of mercy—weeping for a world that, weary, turns away from You. That we might waken & face our fears through the reflection of Your sorrow, all of creation discipling to Your suffering, the shortest path between Heaven & earth. That this city is a beautiful child with downcast eyes—its streets melancholy. Tomorrow, the lemon trees will blossom & the olive trees rejoice—but today, You cry for everything that's nothing, & nothing of what's everything—that love is stronger than strong walls, greater than what cannot be seen.

Only a Branch

John 15:1-11

The fat wet vine curling into my arms is gentle as blue flame & firm & rich & brimming with fruit. It reaches for my body, & I am waiting for it to rise around me as night falls. Untamable by dawn, it envelops me—grows within my lungs, up my throat, & out of my mouth. There is solace in the overgrowth, my leaves so green & lush, & on my tongue one single grape, a humble, joyous fruit, & I am complete.

Run Beloved, Run

Hebrews 12:1-3

I begin to run, my face to the wind, back to the sun; I press forward, heart racing & lungs filled, breathing steady, strides so steep, each step a note, music in flight, rhythm in motion, a discipline, a faith moving forward. I have seen pictures of women running, short legs, long legs, heard marathon stories, begin to use my legs & heart for this, gladly use them up to claw, to fight, to run with grace. Miles in, my lungs bellow & I focus on my body—effort, posture, cadence. My lungs drink deeper & I relax my shoulders, smile at the hurt. Miles & miles in, sweat stings my chafed, raw skin & I force my aching legs to keep moving forward, barely in pace. *I hurt. I hurt. I hurt.* My faith begs me forward for what I hope to find, but the wall I'm about to hit is heavy, like a black rock on my shoulders bigger & older than me. Longing & hoping will not lighten it; success will not shift it. I run hunched over & pray until I am in a place of great beauty & familiarity & the afternoon sun begins to dip behind the hills. I straighten my posture & am upright in a world where there is no weight or pain. I run & I stretch the tendons that hold my spirit together, that I might hear His maddening cheers root me on in this run against distance. & when I finally reach the end, slumped, gasping, glinting with sweat, muscles blazing—having only reached the beginning, I will fall into His arms & His reassurance of a job well done.

The Touch of a Towel

John 13:1-17

You kneel before me, take off my sandals & I feel welcome in Your hands. I am exposed—feet grimy, full of callouses & cracks, pungent with sweat. I pull back but You reassure. In this moment, as You ready the water, You look up & search my eyes. You wash my feet, holding them each in Your hand, one by one, watching the cool water soak away the dirt, Your fingers pressing into my bones & hard skin. I see Your reflection in the ripples of the cleansing, see myself in Your water—who I am & who I can be. These small things—You reaching out Your hand, touching, cleansing—see how such things become mighty when so full of love. This is the way, in these moments, when silence ebbs between us, that we learn we are whole & at home in Your touch. You look to me, to my neighbor, & hand the towel to me.

It Is Finished

John 19:30

& when you said, *It is finished.*—did Your ears still ring with shouts of *Hosanna!* as they scoffed & mocked you; did the crumbs of the bread You'd broken just hours earlier fall from where they'd gathered as they struck You & ripped out Your beard; did the smell of the anointing oil from the day before mingle with the blood flowing from Your thorny crown as You hung broken; did Your hands— now pierced through—remember the healing touch to the servant's ear, just yesterday, in the garden; did the taste of that last supper's wine linger on Your tongue, mixing with the vinegar they thrust to Your lips just moments before You uttered Your last words; did You, when You called out in Your forsakenness look forward to the soon-coming promise You would give; did You—even as You said, *It is finished* & relinquished Your spirit—notice the trembling of earth & heaven; did Your body—even then—ache for its coming reconciliation, resurrection, redemption, & glorification? You, stripped so that we might be clothed, mocked so that we might be honored, broken so that we might be restored, crucified so that we might be given life. *It is finished,* You said. & I can hear You say it, the words almost a whisper, then not even that, but an echo so faint it seems no longer to come from You in Your moment, Your final moment. *It is finished,* You said into a vastness that led to an even greater vastness, & yet all of it within You for us.

He Is Risen

Matthew 28:1-10

May your sight burn with flames of grace as you stand over His body in the tomb before they roll the stone—burn to behold the roaring Spirit having brought Him back to life again. May your despairing heart be singed with joy as He greets you, be nourished by His love surprising you in that morning, as He stands defiant before the world, as the Son of God, having thundered in sackcloth at their disbelief—for He is risen, given us power over death, striven in our place to run the race, is among the living, & has given us grace. & I will rise, open up my life & heart wide, take up my cross, grave open wide, will rise in His light.